C000088200

Cover illustration: A Saab JA 37 Viggen interceptor flown by F13 Wing, Swedish Air Force.

1. The French Dassault Mirage III tailless delta was designed as a Mach 2 all-weather interceptor and first flew as a prototype on 17 November 1956. Several later versions followed the original production model into service with the French and other air forces, each of the more modern examples being powered by a single SNECMA Atar 9C or 9K turbojet. The Swiss Air Force received Mirage III-S fighter-bombers, the example seen here using JATO rockets to assist take-off.

WARBIRDS ILLUSTRATED NO. 28

World Fighters
1945~1985

MICHAEL J. H. TAYLOR

ARMS AND ARMOUR PRESS
London—Melbourne—Harrisburg, Pa.—Cape Town

Introduction

Warbirds Illustrated 28: World Fighters, 1945–1985
Published in 1984 by Arms and Armour Press, Lionel Leventhal Limited, 2–6 Hampstead High Street, London NW3 1QQ; 11 Munro Street, Port Melbourne 3207, Australia; Sanso Centre, 8 Adderley Street, P.O. Box 94, Cape Town 8000, South Africa; Cameron and Kelker Streets, P.O. Box 1831, Harrisburg, Pennsylvania 17105, USA

British Library Cataloguing in Publication Data
Taylor, Michael J. H.
World fighters, 1945–1985—(Warbirds illustrated; 28)
1. Fighter planes—History—Pictorial works
I. Title   II. Series
623.74′64′0222   UG1242.F5
ISBN 0-85368-668-8

Editing and layout by Roger Chesneau. Typeset by CCC, printed and bound in Great Britain by William Clowes Limited, Beccles and London.

Having got to the stage of producing tens of thousands of machines a year, aircraft manufacturers discovered that the military market suddenly collapsed with the Armistice of 1918. Although it cannot be said that the end of the Second World War proved much easier for some companies, two factors ensured that the catastrophic effects of the contract cancellations of 1918 would not be repeated wholesale in 1945. First, the unease between some of the Allied nations of the Second World War came to a head soon after peace returned. New battle-lines formed because of the sharp divisions between the economic and political systems of the former allies; in geographical terms, these met head-on in conquered and divided Germany. The second factor was the advent of the jet fighter and jet bomber, with performances far superior to those of then-conventional aircraft: the major air forces had virtually to abandon deployment of land-based piston fighters, so keeping some manufacturers in full production. The demise of the piston-engined heavy bomber came somewhat later, as the power of early turbojet and turboprop engines was insufficient to cause an immediate end to the production and development of these large warplanes. However, not all production of small piston warplanes ended so quickly, for it was some years before naval aircraft switched to jet power.

The distinction between pure fighters/interceptors and tactical fighters intended for ground attack is often not clearly defined, although for the purposes of this book the word 'fighter' has been taken to mean an aircraft the original role of which was seen as air-to-air combat rather than other military duties. Such a definition is more important today than ever, since even jet trainers can now launch dogfight missiles when scrambled as emergency fighters.

World Fighters 1945–85 illustrates and describes aircraft that entered military service after the end of the Second World War, although one or two wartime machines that continued to be produced after 1945 are included to 'set the scene'.

Michael J. H. Taylor

2. Britain's second jet fighter type was the de Havilland DH.100 Vampire, first flown in 1943. The fuselage nacelle was of plywood/balsa/plywood sandwich construction and housed the single Goblin turbojet engine. The Vampire entered service with the RAF in 1946; the FB.5 shown was a fighter-bomber variant of 1949.

▲3 ▼4

3. First flown in 1936, the Supermarine Spitfire became the most famous fighter aircraft to serve in the Second World War, its unusual wing shape making it easily distinguishable from its Allied and enemy contemporaries. Well over 20,000 were built, the last in 1947. A variant for use from aircraft carriers was the Seafire, the FR.XVII illustrated representing a postwar variant for fighter-reconnaissance duties. On 1 April 1954 the very last RAF Spitfire sortie was flown in Malaya, and in November of that year the Seafire was finally retired. Counted among the 2,550 Seafires, the FR.XVII was Rolls-Royce Griffon powered and had a revised cockpit hood and cut-away rear fuselage decking. (Ministry of Defence)

4. The Chance Vought F4U Corsair naval fighter was ordered into production some months before the United States entered the Second World War, first joining land-based US Marine Corps squadrons before going to sea on board Royal Navy and US Navy aircraft carriers. Production continued until the end of 1952, some aircraft possessing a speed of 470mph (756km/h) on the power of the Wright radial engine. Here Corsairs of the First Marine Aircraft Wing are guided into position by a 'leatherneck' prior to a mission during the Korean War of the early 1950s. (US Marine Corps)

5. Designed originally to a British request, the North American P-51 Mustang proved to be perhaps the finest long-range escort fighter of the Second World War. New variants appeared after the end of the war, and some aircraft, like this Dominican Air Force F-51D, continued in service as fighter-bombers into the 1960s and 1970s. The Packard-engined 'D' had a maximum speed of 437mph (703km/h). (Denis Hughes)

5▼

▲6

6. The Gloster Meteor was the only Allied jet aircraft to become operational as a fighter during the Second World War, first joining the RAF in July 1944. The major postwar version was the Meteor F.8, a four-cannon fighter with a speed of 592mph (956km/h). F.8s flown by the Royal Australian Air Force were the only British jets to see action during the Korean War; shown here are No 77 Squadron RAAF examples, being readied for a mission to strike at supply targets using 'flaming onion' napalm rockets of the squadron's invention. (RAAF)

7. The RAF's first jet-powered night fighter was the Meteor

NF.11, which entered service in 1951. A two-seater developed by Armstrong Whitworth, it featured an extended nose to house AI radar; power was provided by two Rolls-Royce Derwent turbojets. A Flight of NF.11s from RAF West Malling is shown.

8. A large number of Allied and friendly nations took up the Vampire in its many forms. Here, awaiting delivery, are a side-by-side two-seat Vampire trainer for Burma, a de Havilland Venom for Iraq, a Vampire night fighter destined for India and (top) a Vampire fighter for Egypt. The Royal Navy flew a small number of F.20 Sea Vampire fighters.

▼7   8▶

▲9

9. At the end of 1943 Grumman flew the first prototype of a new twin-engined naval fighter-bomber, later named the F7F Tigercat in US Marine Corps and US Navy service. Tigercats were not used operationally until after the war as single-seat fighter-bombers and two-seat night fighters, then mostly by the Marines from land bases but also from *Midway* and *Essex* class aircraft carriers. Production continued until 1946 but postwar service was short. Powered by two Pratt & Whitney R-2800 radial engines, the F7F-3 single-seater (as illustrated) had a speed of 435mph (700km/h) and carried an armament of four cannon and four machine-guns.

10. Postwar-built Grumman F7F-3N and -4N Tigercat night fighters were easily identifiable by their modified fuselage noses that housed radar and by their redesigned vertical tail surfaces. The F7F-4N was the only Tigercat version with carrier deck arrester gear fitted, the very few built representing the US Navy's first carrier fighters with tricycle undercarriages.

11. To the Lockheed P-80 (later F-80) Shooting Star went the honour of becoming the USAAF's first operational jet fighter,

▼10

when production P-80As began equipping units at the end of 1945. Although first flown in prototype form on the power of a British engine in January 1944, Allison J33-powered production Shooting Stars were too late for wartime use but were deployed during the Korean War of the early 1950s. The photograph shows a 580mph (933km/h) F-80C; on 8 November 1950 such an aircraft, flown by Lt. Russel Brown Jr. of the USAF's 51st Fighter-Interceptor Wing, shot down a Chinese MiG-15 over Korea; this was the first ever victory in all-jet air combat.

12. First flown in prototype form in 1944, the de Havilland DH.103 Hornet had been designed as a fighter-bomber for use in the Pacific theatre of war. Too late for wartime use, the RAF received single-seat fighters (with four cannon as fixed armament) plus a few unarmed photographic-reconnaissance aircraft, the former becoming the RAF's last piston-engined fighters. Powered by two Rolls-Royce Merlins, the Hornet demonstrated 472mph (760km/h). The Fleet Air Arm received fighter and two-seat night fighter variants as Sea Hornets, an NF.21 night fighter with an ASH scanner in the modified nose being illustrated.

▲13 ▼14

13. In an attempt to produce a more potent successor to the F6F Hellcat, Grumman developed the F8F Bearcat, a smaller and lighter yet higher-powered single-seat fighter of more modern appearance. First flown in 1944, 421mph (678km/h) production Bearcats were delivered to the US Navy from 1945 for interceptor, night fighter and photographic roles, the last joining units in 1948. Later aircraft were armed with four cannon. All Bearcats had passed out of Navy service by 1952, but the type saw action in Indo-China when ex-US aircraft were flown there by the French. Illustrated is an F8F-2.

14. Reviving the name 'Fury' for a fighter, Hawker developed this single-seat monoplane fighter-bomber for the RAF and the first prototype appeared in 1944. It was exported after the war but not adopted by the RAF, although it became a major service type with the Royal Navy as the four-cannon Sea Fury, joining units in 1947 and serving during the Korean War: powered by a Bristol Centaurus radial engine, which allowed a speed of 460mph (740km/h), it was the FAA's last piston fighter. Here a Sea Fury FB.10 is dropping by lift into a hangar on board HMS *Illustrious*.

15. The first US Navy aircraft to use turbojet power was the Ryan FR-1 Fireball, a single-seat fighter with a conventional radial engine in the nose and a turbojet in the fuselage tail. The sixty-six Fireballs built served until 1947. The US Navy's first pure jet fighter was the McDonnell FH-1 Phantom, first flown in January 1945 and illustrated here. Sixty production aircraft were delivered during 1947–48. Each 505mph (810km/h) Phantom was powered by two Westinghouse J30 turbojets carried in the roots of the straight wings, and fixed armament comprised four machine-guns.

16. A wartime USAAF requirement, for a very long range fighter to escort bombers in action in the Pacific theatre, led to North American's curious P-82 Twin Mustang. Basically two standard single-seat P-51 Mustangs joined by a common centre wing and centre tailplane, only a few had been completed by VJ-Day, but a postwar order produced fighters and night fighters, an F-82 (as redesignated) of the USAF's 68th Fighter Squadron claiming the first enemy aircraft of the Korean War. (US Air Force)

17. Pending the availability of sufficient quantities of jet aircraft to equip first-line fighter squadrons postwar, the Soviet and one or two other air forces deployed piston-engined Yakovlev Yak-9U and -P fighters, North Korean Yak-9Ps operating during the Korean War. Of equal importance were the Lavochkin La-9 fighter and La-11 longer-range escort fighter, both entering Soviet units just too late for wartime use but equipping a number of air forces postwar. The three-cannon La-11, as illustrated, could attain 459mph (740km/h) on the power of its radial piston engine.

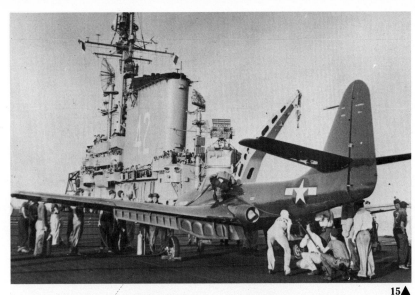

15▲

16▲ 17▼

18. Having achieved great wartime success with its P-47 Thunderbolt, Republic went into jet fighter production with its P-84 (later F-84) Thunderjet, the prototype of which first flew on 28 February 1946. The aircraft was powered by a single Allison J35 turbojet engine and armed initially with six machine-guns, and production in fighter, escort fighter and fighter-bomber variants totalled 4,457. The most numerous version was the F-84G, a 622mph (1,001km/h) fighter-bomber, many of which were supplied to other air forces under a military aid programme. F-84Gs were also the first USAF fighter-bombers able to carry tactical nuclear weapons. The F-84G illustrated in this 1953 photograph was the 4,000th Thunderjet built; alongside is an F-84F Thunderstreak.

19. On 24 April 1946 the Soviet Union joined the small band of nations to have designed and flown their own jet fighters, when both the single Jumo 004B-engined Yakovlev Yak-15 and the twin BMW 003A-engined Mikoyan-Gurevich MiG-9 single-seaters made their first flights. The former was first to enter Soviet service, powered by a developed Jumo engine known as the RD-10. It was basically a Yak-3 with the fuselage modified to accept an underfuselage-exhausting turbojet. Speed was about 488mph (786km/h). The MiG-9 (illustrated) used two RD-20s in production form and was a three-cannon fighter capable of 565mph (910km/h).

20. Republic F-84Ds and F-84Es were operational with the USAF in Korea, the 27th Fighter Escort Wing achieving outstanding combat performance. The F-84E introduced several innovations, including a new Sperry-developed gunsight to compute for aerial and ground gunnery, rocketry and bombing. Here an F-84E blasts eight of its sixteen 5in rockets.

▲21 ▼22

21. Supermarine jet fighters were less successful than their piston predecessors, but they nevertheless established several important 'firsts' in British service. The Attacker, originally intended to be an RAF fighter, first flew as a prototype on 27 July 1946 and eventually became the Fleet Air Arm's first standardized carrier jet fighter. Fighter and fighter-bomber versions were built, entering service from 1951; others went as landplanes to Pakistan. Powered by a Rolls-Royce Nene, the 590mph (950km/h) Attacker had a fixed armament of four cannon. Here the second navalized prototype is seen on board ship for the first time.

22. A Royal Navy Attacker F.1 in production colours.

23. After the German occupation of Czechoslovakia was over, Avia continued to construct various German aircraft it had been forced to build during the war (such as the Messerschmitt Bf 109G), but now for the Czechoslovak Air Force. The company also produced fighters, fighter-bombers and trainers under the S-92/CS-92 designations for the home air force, representing copies of the German Messerschmitt Me 262 jet fighter built largely from components left in the country by the retreating Germans and powered by Jumo 004 engines produced in the Praga engine factory. The first Czech jet fighter flew in August 1946. This CS-92 was photographed in front of a Czech-built MiG-17.

24. It is perhaps surprising that, coming from the same company that had conceived the highly successful F4U Corsair naval piston fighter, Chance Vought's first jet fighter was so uninspiring. The F6U Pirate first flew on 2 October 1946, thirty entering US Navy service from the end of 1949 as four-cannon fighters; each was powered by a Westinghouse J34 turbojet, and these were the first US Navy fighters to use afterburners. A further innovation was the use of Metalite, a newly developed material comprising two thin sheets of aluminium alloy bonded to a core of balsa wood, to skin the airframe. The photograph shows the first prototype Pirate.

▲25

25. To rival Chance Vought's Pirate for US Navy orders, North American produced its own straight-winged jet fighter, the FJ-1 Fury. This adopted the more powerful Allison J35 engine and was armed with six machine-guns. Later proving capable of 547mph (880km/h), the Fury first flew on 27 November 1946 and thirty served with VF-5A on board USS *Boxer*.

26. About the time McDonnell received a US Navy contract to put its Phantom into production, it also received the go-ahead to develop a larger naval carrier fighter. This too emerged as a single-seater with straight wings, but the F2H Banshee used two Westinghouse J34 engines of greater thrust than the Phantom's J30s and was produced in much larger numbers – and in several variants. The first prototype flew on 11 January 1947 and the US Navy began receiving Banshees in 1949 as four-cannon fighters; later versions included night fighters and photographic-reconnaissance aircraft. Here an F2H-3 fighter is launched from USS *Hancock* during steam catapult trials.

27. The US Navy's F2H-3 Banshee was longer by comparison with earlier versions, could carry extra fuel, incorporated search radar in the nose, and could refuel in flight using the probe-and-drogue technique (as seen here from a Convair R3Y Tradewind long-range tanker-transport flying-boat).

▲28

28. Some Banshees lasted with the US Navy into the 1960s (but not in front-line use), becoming F-2 types under the revised designation system. Back in the mid 1950s, thirty-nine ex-US Navy F2H-3s had been sold to the Royal Canadian Navy to fly from the aircraft carrier HMCS *Bonaventure*; three of these are illustrated.

29. Grumman switched from piston to turbojet power for its F9F Panther single-seat fighter. The first prototype, with an imported Rolls-Royce Nene engine installed, made its maiden flight on 24

November 1947. A very large number were built in several versions, most with Pratt & Whitney J42 or J48 engines (the J42 was basically a US-built Nene and the J48 was similar to the British Tay). Deliveries lasted from 1949 to 1952. The Panther was an excellent fighter, the F9F-5 attaining 579mph (932km/h), and all versions were armed with four cannon. Only eight days after the outbreak of the Korean War, F9F-2 Panthers were flown from USS *Valley Forge* against North Korean forces.

▼29

30▲

30. The North American F-86 (originally P-86) Sabre matured from the USAAF's original intention of receiving a straight-winged jet fighter similar to the Navy's FJ-1 Fury which, in 1945, was in the design stage, but by mid-year the USAAF had reviewed the design and it was modified to incorporate swept wings. The first prototype Sabre, powered by an Allison J35 engine, flew on 1 October 1947. This was later re-engined, as was the second aircraft, with a General Electric J47, which became the standard powerplant for the huge number of Sabres built thereafter for US and foreign service. Apart from being the USAF's first swept-wing jet (in 1949), the F-86 was the first jet fighter able to demonstrate a speed of Mach 1. From 17 December 1950 Sabres were flown in action in Korea, the 4th Fighter-Interceptor Wing claiming four MiG-15s on this first day. Illustrated are F-86As. (US National Archives)

31. Six machine-guns plus the usual optional bombs or rockets made up the standard armament of early Sabres. Later aircraft used four cannon in place of the machine-guns, with the exception of the F-86D. This version (illustrated), first flown in December 1949 and the major production model, carried radar in the nose and had as its fixed armament a retractable pack of twenty-four 2.75in 'Mighty Mouse' unguided air-to-air rockets.

31▼

▲32

▲33

32. Apart from US F-86 production, F-86Ks were assembled in Italy; in Australia, where the Commonwealth Aircraft Corporation produced the CA-27 (a Rolls-Royce Avon-powered Sabre for the RAAF); and in Canada by Canadair. Canadian-built J47-engined Sabres went to the RCAF, the USAF and, as an interim fighter, the RAF, and production also included CL-13 Sabres, fitted with Canadian-developed Orenda turbojet engines, for service in the RCAF and the air forces of West Germany, South Africa and Colombia. The Orenda turbojet of this CL-13 is being exposed for inspection.
33. Although Australian Avon-engined Sabres were the fastest of all models, attaining around 700mph (1,125km/h) compared to the F-86F's 687mph (1,105km/h) on the power of a J47, they were the least numerous. These Canadian-built Sabres were among those operated by the Luftwaffe.
34. RAF Sabres built in Canada were operational from 1953 to 1956, thereafter passing to Greece, Italy, Turkey and Yugoslavia.
35. A fly-past of Canadair-built Sabres of the RCAF.

36. One of the least known production jet fighters was the Swedish Saab-21R, a direct jet development of the Saab-21 'pusher' piston-engined fighter. First flown with a British Goblin turbojet engine on 10 March 1947, the Saab-21R entered Swedish Air Force service from 1950, the sixty J 21RA and RB fighters each having one cannon and four Bofors guns as fixed armament.

Later, with the appearance of the purpose-designed Saab-29 jet fighter, the J21s were assigned new attack roles as A 21Rs, as seen here firing rockets.

37. A formation of three Lockheed F-80B Shooting Star fighters. The 'B' variant featured a better gun armament, a more powerful version of the J33 engine and thinner wings than the P-80A.

▼36

▲38

38. The Soviet-built MiG-15 was one of the major fighters of the Korean War. This MiG-15 fell into USAF hands and was taken to Okinawa for examination and flight testing. (US National Archives)

▼39

39. No. 5 Sqn Lightning F.6 interceptors, the machine nearest the camera carrying the latest colour scheme. (John Jackson, Louth)

40. A Grumman F9F-8 Cougar.

40▶

▲41 ▼42

43▲

41. The final version of the Lockheed F-104 Starfighter was the F-104S, an Aeritalia-developed fighter-bomber based on the F-104G but with an uprated J79 engine and Sparrow/Sidewinder missile armament. F-104S Starfighters went into Italian and Turkish service.

42. An Israeli IAI Kfir-C2 being prepared with attack and self-defence armament.

43. The USAF's great rival in the air war over Korea was the Soviet swept-winged Mikoyan-Gurevich MiG-15, a less sophisticated jet fighter but with a higher rate of climb and a better turning circle at high altitudes. Its performance can be attributed mainly to its original RD-45 and later Klimov VK-1 engines, both direct developments of the British Rolls-Royce

Nene (twenty-five examples of which had been sent to the USSR from Britain in 1947, along with thirty Derwents). The first I-310 prototype flew on 2 July 1947, followed by the second with a Nene engine on 30 December. Three-cannon MiG-15s entered Soviet service in 1948, and improved versions included the 668mph (1,076km/h) MiG-15bis. Others went to China and North Korea, the illustrated aircraft being a North Korean MiG that was flown to the USAF base at Kimpo on 21 September 1953 by a defecting pilot after the end of the Korean War. (US Air Force)

44. MiG-15 variants were also built in Poland and Czechoslovakia: Polish Air Force LiM-2s (MiG-15bis) are seen here. China also built hundreds as its first production jet aircraft. (Polish Air Force)

44▼

◀47

45. First flown as a prototype all-weather single-seat fighter in March 1948, the Douglas F3D Skynight subsequently joined US Navy and Marine squadrons and fought in Korea, recording the first destruction at night of an enemy jet fighter (a MiG-15) on 2 November 1952. The major production version was the USMC's F3D-2, a 600mph (965km/h) fighter using two Westinghouse J34 turbojet engines. Some Skynights were modified into missile carriers with the letter 'M' as a suffix to the designation, the usual four cannon then being relegated by Sparrows (as shown).

46. Northrop's F-89 Scorpion was a two-seat all-weather interceptor fighter, featuring straight wings and two Allison J35 engines. The prototype, which first flew on 16 August 1948, was followed by several production versions for the USAF's Air Defense Command, with initial operational deployment in 1951. The main differences between the versions was in armament, the six cannon and wingtip fuel tanks on early versions giving way on the F-89D to new wingtip pods carrying fuel and fifty-two 2.75in air-to-air rockets. F-89Hs, as illustrated (with the centre aircraft using afterburning), had a further pod change to house three retractable Hughes Falcon missiles and twenty-one rockets on each wing.

47. The F-89D was the fastest version of the Scorpion, attaining 610mph (982km/h). From the mid 1950s, aircraft of this model were modified to F-89J type, losing some speed but gaining the ability to launch two Douglas MB-1 Genie nuclear air-to-air unguided missiles, plus four Falcons carried under the wings and rockets in the wingtip pods. This F-89J has both Genie and Falcon missiles under its wings.

▲48 ▼49

32

50▲

51▲

48. Europe's first fully swept-wing jet fighter was the remarkable Swedish Saab-29, which first flew as a prototype on 1 September 1948 and joined the Flygvapnet in several versions as a day fighter, attack aircraft and photographic-reconnaissance type from 1951. Each version was powered by an SFA RM2 turbojet, a licence-built Rolls-Royce Ghost, the final J 29F fighter (as shown) using an afterburner to boost speed to 659mph (1,060km/h). The standard fixed armament of the J 29 fighter was four cannon, although later the J 29F (newly built aircraft and earlier examples brought to this standard) also carried Sidewinder missiles.

49. Production line of Saab-29s. In five years more than 660 were built for the Swedish Air Force. A small number of ex-Swedish J 29Fs were passed to Austria.

50. Britain achieved notable success with the Sea Hawk, a single-seat carrier fighter that also went into service with the navies of West Germany, India and the Netherlands. Indeed, Indian Sea Hawks were only superseded on board the carrier *Vikrant* in the early 1980s. Produced in several versions for interceptor fighter and fighter-bomber duties, the Sea Hawk had first flown as a Hawker prototype on 3 September 1948 and Hawker-built production aircraft joined the Royal Navy in 1953. Later aircraft were built by Armstrong Whitworth. WF145 was the third Sea Hawk F.1 and is seen here on board HMS *Eagle*, the first carrier to embark the type.

51. All versions of the Sea Hawk used the Rolls-Royce Nene turbojet engine and the standard fixed armament was four cannon, although this was supplemented on later models by rockets, bombs and Sidewinder missiles. This Sea Hawk FGA.6 fighter-bomber carries ten rockets and two 500lb bombs in addition to drop tanks.

33

▲52

▲53 ▼54

52. To the Sea Hawk went the distinction of being the first RN interceptor with folding wings, as clearly demonstrated by this F.1. Note the Westland Dragonfly helicopter overhead.

53. No. 806 Squadron, FAA, was the first to receive Sea Hawks, one of its F.1s being seen here landing on board HMS *Eagle*. However, although *Eagle* was one of three British carriers used during the 1956 Suez Crisis, No 806 did not participate.

54. The German Navy received more than sixty Sea Hawks, half as day fighters and half as all-weather fighters. Here, three aircraft destined for Germany start their engines at Bitteswell airfield in preparation for a flight to Bremen.

55. The F7U-3 Cutlass appeared in three versions, the standard fighter, the F7U-3M missile carrier with provision for four Sparrows, and the F7U-3P photographic-reconnaissance aircraft.

Armament for the standard fighter was four cannon plus 'Mighty Mouse' air-to-air unguided rockets. This Cutlass from VA-83 makes a touch-and-go landing on board the British carrier *Eagle* during NATO exercise 'Maltex 56' in 1956.

56. As a follow-up design to the Pirate, Chance Vought produced the F7U Cutlass. This was a uniquely configured single-seat fighter with swept wings carrying twin vertical tail units and combined ailerons and elevators known then as ailavators. The first prototype made its maiden flight on 29 September 1948 and was followed by Westinghouse J34-powered F7U-1 evaluation aircraft. Major production came with the enlarged F7U-3, powered by two, more powerful Westinghouse J46s, bestowing a speed of 680mph (1,094km/h). These F7U-3 Cutlass fighters served with VF-124 at the US Naval Air Station at Miramar.

55▼

56▼

▲57 ▼58

59▲

60▲

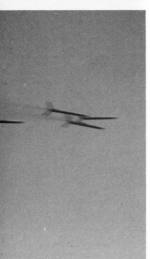

57. The USAF's first all-weather jet fighter was the Lockheed F-94 Starfire, a tandem two-seat radar-equipped aircraft related to the company's T-33 trainer. Initial production aircraft, designated F-94As, entered service in 1950 and these, plus the following F-94Bs, were powered by Allison J33 turbojet engines. The most important version, however, was the F-94C (shown), which was capable of 585mph (941km/h).

58. The F-94A and F-94B were each armed with four machine-guns, but the Pratt & Whitney J-48-powered F-94C was a much more refined aircraft and carried twenty-four 'Mighty Mouse' air-to-air unguided rockets in the fuselage nose, packed around the radome, and a further forty-eight in two wing pods.

59. As a successor to its Vampire, de Havilland produced the similarly configured DH.112 Venom. Despite its similarity, however, this was virtually a new design, and operated on the much higher-rated de Havilland Ghost engine. Speed was 640mph (1,030km/h) for the initial production FB.1. Carrying four cannon plus bombs or rockets, Venoms served with the RAF as single-seat fighter-bombers and two-seat night fighters from 1952, an NF.3 night fighter being illustrated. Venoms were also produced in Switzerland.

60. The carrier-borne naval counterpart to the Venom was the Sea Venom, a two-seater flown by the Fleet Air Arm and the Royal Australian Navy as their first all-weather jet fighter. The final Sea Venom variant for the FAA, the F(AW).22, was also the first missile-carrying variant, equipped to launch two Firestreaks.

▲61 ▼62

61. The first production jet fighter of French original design was the Dassault MD 450 Ouragan. This single-seater attained 585mph (941km/h) on the power of a single Hispano-built Rolls-Royce Nene turbojet engine and had four cannon as its fixed armament. It was first flown on 28 February 1949, and the French Air Force received 350 full production fighters from the early 1950s, others going to India and Israel. (Ministère des Armées 'Air')

62. Although the MiG-15 had proved to be an outstanding fighter during the Korean War, several of its shortcomings were recognized and an attempt to remedy these produced the similar MiG-17. A VK-1- or VK-1A-powered single-seater capable of 711mph (1,145km/h) and armed progressively with three more potent cannon and 'Alkali' missiles, the MiG-17 joined Soviet units from 1953 as a day fighter and later as an all-weather interceptor. Czechoslovakia, Poland and China also produced MiG-17s, and this Egyptian example was among the large number exported to many foreign air forces. (Denis Hughes)

63. As a swept-wing development of the F-84 Thunderjet,

Republic produced the 658mph (1,058km/h) F-84F Thunderstreak, powered by an Armstrong Siddeley Sapphire ASSa 3 turbojet engine produced under licence by Wright in the USA. The initial prototype first flew on 3 June 1950 and six-gun production Thunderstreaks went to USAF units as fighter-bombers and bomber escorts from 1954, later joining eight other NATO air forces. USAF Thunderstreaks based in the UK were assigned to spearhead NATO's nuclear retaliation should war break out in Europe.

64. The first and only production jet fighter to originate in Canada was the Avro CF-100. A tandem two-seater flown as a prototype on 19 January 1950, it was the first straight-winged combat aircraft to demonstrate Mach 1 performance (in a dive) and was produced in several versions for the RCAF and Belgian Air Force. Power was provided by two Orenda turbojets and armament differed according to version between six machine-guns and/or air-to-air rockets. CF-100 Mk 3s that entered service from 1953 and represented the first production version, were the RCAF's first all-weather jet fighters. This is a Mk 4.

▲65

65. On 23 February 1951 the prototype of a new French swept-wing fighter to supersede the Ouragan flew as the Dassault MD 452 Mystère. Standardizing on the SNECMA Atar 101 turbojet engine, production Mystère IICs entered French Air Force service from 1954. A developed version was the Mystère IVA, which was built for French, Indian and Israeli service, powered by Hispano-built Rolls-Royce Tay or Hispano-Suiza Verdon 350 engines and capable of speeds of up to 695mph (1,118km/h). Illustrated is the Mystère IVB, which was built in limited numbers and featured new radar and engine afterburning.

66. The only production version of the Douglas Skyray for the US Navy and Marines was the F4D-1, a 695mph (1,118km/h) interceptor powered by a single Pratt & Whitney J57 turbojet engine. It had delta-type wings with rounded tips and swept trailing edges and was armed with four cannon plus optional underwing missiles and other weapons. The prototype first flew on 23 January 1951 and deliveries took place between 1956 and 1959. These Skyrays were operated by VMF-115.

67. First flown as a prototype on 20 July 1951, the Hawker Hunter single-seat day fighter entered RAF service from 1954 and is seen by many as the ultimate development of the subsonic jet fighter. Capable of 715mph (1,150km/h) and armed with either four cannon or cannon and ground attack weapons, most production Hunters used the Rolls-Royce Avon turbojet although the Armstrong Siddeley Sapphire powered a small number. Nearly 2,000 were produced, including some built in Belgium and the Netherlands, and many were exported. Today the Hunter remains a much-prized fighter-bomber, the Swiss Air Force alone operating some 140 refurbished F.58s. These Hunter F.6s were flown by No 208 Squadron, RAF. (Ministry of Defence)

67▼

68. RAF Hunter F(GA).9s of No 20 Squadron, RAF, on an anti-infiltration patrol over Malaysian territory.

69. A Swiss Air Force Hunter F.58.

◀69

▲70

70. The Supermarine Swift was the RAF's first swept-wing interceptor-fighter. The prototype flew on 5 August 1951 and production Swifts entered service from 1953 but were soon withdrawn. Only the FR.5 fighter-reconnaissance aircraft achieved longer service, remaining operational from 1956 to 1961. Each Swift was powered by a single Rolls-Royce Avon engine, the 685mph (1,102km/h) FR.5 carrying two cannon and optionally eight air-to-surface rockets as well as cameras. The Swift FR.5s illustrated belonged to No 2 Squadron.

71. McDonnell's first swept-wing production fighter was the F3H Demon for the US Navy, a single-seater for carrier operations. It was first flown as a prototype on 7 August 1951, production examples being four-cannon fighters, cannon and attack weapon strike fighters, and Sparrow III or Sidewinder missile-armed all-weather and night fighters. Here F3H-2N Demons are being launched from USS *Forrestal* on a night training mission. (US National Archives)

72. A USAF pilot puts an F-15 Eagle through its paces.

▼71   72▶

73. Two Royal Navy Sea Harrier V/STOL combat aircraft.

▲74 ▼75

74. A US Navy F-14A Tomcat armed with four Phoenix, two Sparrow and two Sidewinder missiles.
75. Two F-16 Fighting Falcons of the 388th Tactical Fighter Wing, USAF, on a training mission over the Utah Desert.
76. Although the first Demons delivered to the US Navy each had a single Westinghouse J40 turbojet, most Demons operated on the power of the higher-rated Allison J71, as shown. Demons in use during the 1960s were redesignated F-3s. Maximum speed was 647mph (1,041km/h).

77. As a direct development of the excellent F9F Panther, Grumman produced the Cougar. The main updates were the use of swept wings and a higher-rated Pratt & Whitney J48 engine. First flown on 20 September 1951, production covered F9F-6, -7 and -8 single-seat carrier fighters, plus some reconnaissance examples, and these went to US Navy and Marine units from 1952. Here Navy Panthers are being flight-refuelled from a Tradewind flying-boat.

▲78 ▼79

78. The original armament of the Cougar was four cannon but later some were given four Sidewinder missiles, as shown in this view of an F9F-8. Maximum speed of the F9F-8 was 690mph (1,110km/h).

79. On 26 November 1951 Gloster flew the prototype of what was to be its second and final production jet fighter, the Javelin. A tandem two-seater with all-weather capability and powered by two Sapphire turbojet engines, it was the world's first twin-turbojet delta-winged aircraft. Early versions like these initial production F(AW).1s, which entered RAF service in 1956, were armed with four cannon.

80. The first version of the Javelin to be missile-armed was the F(AW).7, which had two cannon and four Firestreaks. This is the first F(AW).7. The Mk 7 became the Mk 9 when fitted with engine reheat and flight-refuelling equipment, attaining 620mph (998km/h).

▲81

▲82

81. On 16 October 1952 the prototype of a new French combat aircraft flew as the SNCASO SO 4050 Vautour. With swept mid-mounted wings carrying two SNECMA Atar 101 engines, the Vautour entered production as the IIN two-seat night fighter, IIA single-seat ground attack aircraft and IIB two-seat bomber. Only 70 IINs were completed for the French Air Force, each capable of 685mph (1,102km/h) and armed with four cannon plus Matra R511 missiles or rockets.

82. North American, which had achieved success with its straight-winged Fury for the US Navy and swept-wing Sabre for the USAF, produced its first swept-wing fighter for the USMC and Navy as the the FJ-2 Fury; the prototype flew on 14 February 1952. FJ-2s used General Electric J47 engines but later FJ-3s (as illustrated) and -4s used Wright J65s, the FJ-4B attaining 680mph (1,094km/h). Late Furies were armed with four cannon plus four Sidewinder missiles. Those Furies remaining in 1962 were redesignated F-1s.

83. As the follow-up to its Saab-29, this Swedish manufacturer flew the prototype Saab-32 Lansen on 3 November 1952. As is still the practice in Sweden for major combat aircraft, the Lansen was produced for fighter, attack and reconnaissance roles, J 32B all-weather and night fighters equipping seven squadrons from 1958. An SFA-built Avon turbojet, known as the RM.6A, powered the fighter, which was armed with four cannon plus four Sidewinder missiles or other weapons. Capable of Mach 1 in a shallow dive, the J 32B had an official maximum speed of 710mph (1,142km/h).

◀83

84. In the 1950s the United States produced six types of fighter aircraft in the so-called 'Century Series', these equipping USAF front-line units for much of the 1950s and 1960s and then on into the next decade. The first 'Century Series' fighter was the North American F-100 Super Sabre, a supersonic aircraft that bore little relationship to the earlier F-86 Sabre. The initial prototype first flew on 25 May 1953. The USAF received F-100A day fighters armed with four cannon, followed by F-100C fighter-bombers, the major production F-100D, and F-100F two-seat trainers. Here, photographed in 1954, are F-100As awaiting delivery at North American's Los Angeles plant.

85. The F-100D Super Sabre introduced four Sidewinder air-to-air missiles to supplement the cannon and could attain 864mph (1,390km/h) on the power of a single Pratt & Whitney J57 turbojet engine. At one time or another Denmark, France, Taiwan and Turkey also flew Super Sabres. Here F-100As of the 479th Fighter Day Wing from George AFB, California, streak supersonically over the desert.

84▲

85▶

▲86

▲87 ▼88

54

86. In September 1953 the Soviet Mikoyan bureau flew the prototype of a new single-seat fighter, designated I-360. Production MiG-19 day fighters, with two Mikulin AM-5F engines and three cannon, entered Soviet units from 1955, becoming their first supersonic fighters (Mach 1.1). More refined and capable versions followed as limited all-weather fighters and fighter-bombers, the MiG-19PM introducing four 'Alkali' air-to-air missiles. Production was also undertaken in Poland and Czechoslovakia: a Czech aircraft is illustrated.

87. Soviet production of the MiG-19 ended in the 1950s, but since the early 1960s China has built its own version, known as the J-6. Capable of Mach 1.45 on the power of Shenyang Wopen-6 turbojets, J-6s equip about forty Chinese regiments, and exports have been made under the F-6 designation. The F-6s illustrated are in Pakistan Air Force service. (John Fricker)

88. Convair's first contribution to the USAF's 'Century Series' was the F-102 Delta Dagger, a delta-winged interceptor-fighter powered by a single Pratt & Whitney J57. The only production single-seat version was the F-102A, which served for many years from 1956 with Air Defense Command. Capable of 825mph (1,327km/h), Delta Daggers were the first USAF fighters built without guns or cannon, instead relying entirely on internally

stowed Falcon missiles and rockets. With its drag-chute billowing, this Delta Dagger lands at Tan Son Nhut Air Base in Vietnam after a mission, in 1966.

89. The third of America's 'Century Series' fighters to fly was the Lockheed F-104 Starfighter, sometimes nicknamed 'the manned missile' because of its configuration (a slim, pointed fuselage married to thin, very short-span wings) and its incredible performance. The prototype first flew on 7 February 1954, but only a relatively small number of aircraft joined the USAF's Air Defense Command and Tactical Air Command. It took the development of the F-104 multi-mission version to get Starfighters into widespread service, this variant becoming a major European combat plane (with European production), and the type was produced also in Canada and Japan. These RCAF CF-104s were built by Canadair and each had an Orenda-built General Electric J79 engine.

90. The J79-powered F-104G is capable of 1,450mph (2,330km/h) and is armed with cannon and missiles. Partners in NATO, two F-104Gs of the Royal Netherlands Air Force from Leeuwarden here fly with USAF F-4E Phantom IIs of the 32nd Tactical Fighter Squadron in Europe. (US Air Force)

▲91

▲92 ▼93

91. Perhaps Grumman's least successful fighter for the US Navy was the F11F Tiger. Developed from the Panther and capable of 750mph (1,207km/h) on the power of its single Wright J65 engine, it was first flown as a prototype on 30 July 1954; subsequent production aircraft had been withdrawn from first-line use by 1959, but Tigers remained in service long enough to receive the new designation F-11A in 1962. Armament was four cannon and four Sidewinder missiles.

92. McDonnell's contribution to the USAF's 'Century Series' was the F-101 Voodoo, first flown as a prototype on 29 September 1954. Powered by two Pratt & Whitney J57 turbojets and capable of 1,220mph (1,963km/h), it joined the USAF's Tactical Air Command in single-seat F-101A and -C forms; the F-101B tandem two-seat all-weather interceptor joined Air Defense Command (also as TF-101B trainer). To replace CF-100s, the RCAF received ex-USAF F-101Bs as CF-101s, which are only now being superseded by Hornets. These were equipped to carry Genie nuclear and Falcon air-to-air missiles.

93. Dassault followed its production of the Mystère with the Super Mystère B-2, an Atar 101G-powered fighter capable of 743mph (1,195km/h) and armed with two cannon plus air-to-air rockets and missiles. The French Air Force received most of the 180 aircraft produced, although some were acquired by Israel. The latter were the last in service: in 1977 twelve were sent to Honduras in refurbished form with Pratt & Whitney J52 engines.

94. On 11 August 1954 a British manufacturer, Folland Aircraft, flew its prototype Midge lightweight fighter; from this was developed the slightly larger Gnat, which first flew on 18 July 1955. Powered by a single Bristol Orpheus 701 engine and armed with two cannon plus bombs or rockets, the Mach 0.98 Gnat entered service as a single-seater with the Indian and Finnish air forces (an example from the latter is shown). A development of the Gnat is still in production in India as the HAL Ajeet; two-seat Gnats were used as trainers in the Royal Air Force – and equipped the *Red Arrows* – for many years.

95. On 25 March 1955 the first prototype Chance Vought F8U (later redesignated F-8) Crusader air superiority fighter flew. Designed for the US Navy, it featured a unique variable-incidence wing to assist in keeping take-off and landing speeds low while retaining a level fuselage for easier carrier deck operation. The US Navy received a large number in day, limited all-weather and all-weather forms, all powered by the Pratt & Whitney J57 turbojet. The F-8E, also flown by the French Navy, had a speed of 1,322mph (2,127km/h) and was armed with four cannon plus four Sidewinder missiles. Only those flown by the French Navy and ex-US aircraft used by the Philippines Air Force remain as first-line fighters today. Illustrated are two F8U-1s (F-8As) of VF-32 on board USS *Saratoga*, the first Navy deployment, each aircraft capable of carrying two Sidewinders in addition to its four cannon and 32 rockets.

▲96 ▼97

98▲

99▲

96. Although belonging to the 'Century Series', Republic's F-105 Thunderchief was put into USAF service as a fighter-bomber powered by a single Pratt & Whitney J75 engine. Capable of 1,385mph (2,230km/h) in developed form, it could be armed with Sidewinder missiles in addition to a heavy attack load of conventional or nuclear weapons and its standard cannon. These F-105Bs of Tactical Air Command were photographed in 1959, having entered service the previous year.

97. Saab's unique double delta-winged Draken was first flown as a prototype on 25 October 1955, entering Swedish Air Force service as an interceptor in 1960. The main production version was the J 35F (illustrated), a Mach 2 aircraft powered by a single R.M.6C (Avon) engine and armed with one cannon and four Saab-built Falcon missiles. Other countries to operate Drakens were Finland and Denmark. (I. Thuresson)

98. One of the first new aircraft to fly in 1956 was the Supermarine Scimitar, a carrier-borne naval interceptor and strike aircraft which served in front-line Fleet Air Arm squadrons from 1958 until 1965. Powered by two Rolls-Royce Avon turbojets, the 710mph (1,143km/h) Scimitar F.1 carried four cannon plus 96 air-to-air rockets or, later, four Sidewinder missiles, and was the FAA's first swept-wing aircraft. Here Scimitars of No 800 Squadron overfly Lossiemouth.

99. The prototype of the Mikoyan MiG-21 first flew on 16 June 1956. It had been developed to supersede earlier swept-wing Soviet fighters and emphasis had been placed on small size, light weight, good handling at both transonic and supersonic speeds, and a high rate of climb. Initial production of the MiG-21 concentrated on a twin-cannon day fighter, but this was followed by many refined versions showing much improved performance and missile, all-weather and multi-mission capability. Indeed, the MiG-21 became the world's most widely used jet fighter, operated by many air forces. Typical of modern versions is the Mach 2.1 MiG-21MF, powered by a Tumansky R-13-300 turbojet engine and armed with cannon and four missiles for an air combat role. Production of the MiG-21 has also been undertaken in Czechoslovakia, China and India.

▲100

▲101　▼102

103▲

104▲

100. To power a new version of its F-102 Delta Dagger, intended as a more powerful all-weather interceptor, Convair selected the Pratt & Whitney J75 turbojet engine. This necessitated structural changes, resulting in the new designation and name F-106 Delta Dart. The area-ruling of the F-106 fuselage was more pronounced, and an easy point of identification was the square-tipped tailfin. Capable of 1,525mph (2,455km/h) and armed with one Genie or Super Genie and four Super Falcon missiles, the F-106A went into Air Defense Command service from 1959. Many of these aircraft, plus F-106B two-seaters, remained in USAF and Air National Guard service in the early 1980s, cannon having been added as one of several updates.

101. As with many other single-seat combat aircraft, specialized two-seat training versions of the Mirage III that retain operational capability have been produced; here, for example, a two-seat Mirage III-DE is seen in Spanish markings. Although still in production, the Mirage III has undergone metamorphosis into a fighter for the late 1980s and onwards, the Mirage 3 NG (Nouvelle Génération) having appeared in prototype form in 1982.

102. The de Havilland Sea Vixen first flew as a naval two-seat, carrier-borne all-weather interceptor-fighter prototype on 20 March 1957, having originally been designed as a land-based fighter for the RAF. A twin-boom aircraft powered by two Rolls-Royce Avon turbojets, the subsonic Sea Vixen entered FAA service from 1959. Fixed armament for the initial F(AW).1 version (shown) comprised twenty-eight 2in rockets in underfuselage packs, supplemented by up to four Firestreak

missiles or other weapons. This variant was followed by the longer-range F(AW).2, Red Top missiles replacing Firestreaks.

103. From its P.1B prototype (first flown on 4 April 1957), English Electric developed and produced the Lightning. This single-seat all-weather fighter entered service in its earliest forms from 1960, becoming the RAF's first fully supersonic fighter. Seen here are two Lightning F.1s from No. 74 ('Tiger') Squadron. These and subsequent versions were each given two Rolls-Royce Avon turbojets with afterburning and sharply swept wings. Today the RAF still deploys a number of Lightning F.6s as interceptors, each capable of Mach 2 and possessing a very high rate of climb. Armament comprises two Red Top or Firestreak missiles or air-to-air rockets, in addition to two optional guns. Kuwait and Saudi Arabia also received Lightnings.

104. Undoubtedly the most important Western fighter of the 1960s and 1970s was the McDonnell Douglas F-4 Phantom II, production of which totalled over 5,000 for the US armed services and for the air forces of many NATO and other countries. In the 1980s it remains a major combat aircraft, although its importance as a fighter to the US forces has been degraded by the appearance of more modern replacements. Originally designed as a two-seat naval long-range attack aircraft, its role was changed to that of a missile fighter before the first prototype flew on 27 May 1958. Initial versions were the F-4A and -B for the US Navy and USMC, and the F-4C for the USAF, each with two General Electric J79 turbojets and capable of Mach 2. Here US Navy F-4Bs share a deck with A-4 Skyhawks (left) and a Douglas Skywarrior.

▲105

105. Foreign operators of the Phantom II include the RAF, which currently deploys the type as an interceptor and fighter-bomber. This service also took over ex-Royal Navy F-4Ks when the last of the Navy's big aircraft carriers was scrapped. Here RAF Phantom FGR.2s (F-4Ms) sweep over the coast armed with Sparrow missiles and rocket pods. British aircraft are powered by Rolls-Royce Spey turbofan engines.

106. USAF F-4Ds and multi-role F-4Es refuel from a Boeing KC-135 tanker.

107. On 30 July 1959 Northrop flew the prototype of a low-cost, lightweight, single-seat supersonic fighter. This was ordered in quantity by the Department of Defense – mainly for supply to other nations under mutual aid programmes – resulting in the 925mph (1,488km/h) single-seat F-5A tactical fighter, the RF-5A photo-reconnaissance aircraft and the F-5B two-seat operational trainer. Each was powered by two General Electric J85 turbojets;

the F-5A is armed with two Sidewinders plus attack weapons if required. Many remain in use today. Uprated versions were introduced as the F-5E and two-seat F-5F Tiger II in the early 1970s, the single-seater being capable of Mach 1.64. These Turkish F-5As are at the 1st Jet Fighter Base at Bandirma.

108. The Indian single-seat HAL HF-24 Marut was the first supersonic fighter to be designed in Asia outside the USSR. Involved in its early development was Professor Kurt Tank, designer of the wartime German Fw 190 fighter. The Marut first flew on 17 June 1961, and entered Indian service from 1964. Two Rolls-Royce Orpheus 703 turbojets allowed Mach 1.02 to be attained, and the armament comprised four cannon and 48 rockets for the air combat role. A tandem two-seat operational trainer version without rocket armament, the Mk 1T, was also built. The Marut is no longer in front-line Indian Air Force service.

106▲

107▲ 108▼

▲109

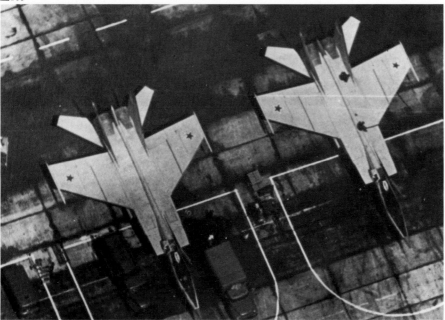

▲110

109. After its Yak-15, Yakovlev produced the similar Yak-17 and Yak-23 single-seat fighters, followed by the two-seat all-weather Yak-25 and improved Yak-27. In 1961 a successor to the Yak-25 and -27 was seen during a fly-past – the missile-carrying Mach 1.8 Yak-28P, examples of which continue in use today with the Soviet interceptor force. A contemporary of the Yak-28P is the Tupolev Tu-28P, the largest interceptor put into operational service by any air force. Powered by two engines, it has a maximum speed of about Mach 1.75 and very long range, and is seen here carrying four 'Ash' missiles.

110. The fastest interceptor ever put into operational service is the Soviet Mikoyan MiG-25, known to the West by the reporting name 'Foxbat'. It was originally designed to counter a Mach 3 cruise bomber then being developed in the USA, and its performance was such that when the bomber was cancelled work on the MiG continued. First flying in the early 1960s, the initial version to enter service was the 'Foxbat-A' single-seat interceptor, capable of Mach 3.2 on its two Tumansky R-31 turbojets but Mach 2.83 when carrying four 'Acrid' missiles. Subsequent versions have included reconnaissance aircraft and converted 'Foxbat-As' for low-altitude interceptor duties, whilst some aircraft have also been exported. A more potent development has been produced as the MiG-31 'Foxhound'.

111. The Mikoyan MiG-23 is a single-seat swing-wing fighter, first seen in public in 1967. Known to the West by the reporting name 'Flogger', it has taken over from the MiG-21 as the main Soviet combat aircraft with tactical and interceptor forces and has been exported. Many versions have appeared, the major production MiG-23MF variant being capable of Mach 2.35 on the power of a single Tumansky R-29 turbojet and carrying a twin-barrel cannon plus six 'Aphid' and 'Apex' missiles. This Soviet MiG-23MF deploying its braking parachute visited Sweden in 1981. (Swedish Air Force)

112. Breaking from its traditional delta

◀111

112▲ 113▼

configurations, Dassault developed a new single-seat all-weather interceptor for the French Air Force and for export as the swept-wing Mirage F1. The prototype first flew on 23 December 1966 and production F1-Cs entered French service from 1973. Other versions include the F1-B two-seat trainer and F1-E multi-role and F1-R reconnaissance aircraft. The F1-C is powered by a SNECMA Atar 9K-50 turbojet, which bestows a speed of Mach 2.2. Armament consists of two cannon plus two Super 530 and two 550 Magic or Sidewinder missiles.

113. An early example of the Saab 37 Viggen, a unique Mach 2 single-seat, all-weather, multi-purpose combat aircraft with rear-mounted wings and delta foreplanes, seen here taking off from a public road during an exercise. First flown as a prototype on 8 February 1967, the Viggen has joined the Swedish Air Force in attack (AJ 37), interceptor (JA 37), photo-reconnaissance (SF 37), maritime reconnaissance (SH 37) and two-seat training (SK 37) forms.

▲114

▲115

114. In 1956 a new Soviet single-seat all-weather fighter was seen in the skies over Moscow. This, the delta-winged Sukhoi Su-9, became operational with the Soviet Air Force, and an improved model, also powered by a single Lyulka AL-7F turbojet, later joined it as the Su-11. Neither aircraft is now used in any numbers, and the current Sukhoi delta is the Su-15 (illustrated), known in the West as 'Flagon'. First seen in public in 1967, this Mach 2.5 twin-jet interceptor has been produced in five versions and carries cannon and four missiles. The Voyska PVO has some 700 Su-15s in service. (Tass)

115. Following a temporary embargo on the delivery of Mirage fighters to Israel, IAI (Israel Aircraft Industries) decided to develop its own delta fighter based on the Mirage and fitted with the Atar 9C turbojet. The resulting aircraft was named the Nesher, which first flew in 1969 and entered air force service. In a more ambitious project, IAI followed the Nesher with the Kfir, and then the refined Kfir-C2 with foreplanes and, most recently, the Kfir-C7. Each Kfir uses a General Electric J79 turbojet to attain a speed of more than Mach 2.3, and armament is two cannon plus Shafrir 2 air-to-air missiles or ground attack weapons, although the aircraft has a varied weapon carrying capability, as shown here. The Colombian Air Force also flies Kfir-C2s.

116. Today, the US Navy's most powerful carrier-based fighter is the two-seat Grumman F-14 Tomcat, a swing-wing, twin-fin aircraft capable of tracking up to 24 enemy targets at once and simultaneously attacking six of them with very long range Phoenix missiles. Sparrows or Sidewinders can also be carried, and in addition the Tomcat has considerable ground attack capabilities. Flown as a prototype on 21 December 1970, the F-14A first entered service in 1972 with VF-1 and VF-2; land-based F-14As were exported to Iran. The Tomcat is powered by two Pratt & Whitney TF30-P-412A turbofan engines and has a maximum speed of Mach 2.34.

117. The USAF's most powerful fighter is currently the McDonnell Douglas F-15 Eagle, a mighty single-seat air superiority fighter with a secondary attack role. Capable of attaining a speed of more than Mach 2.5 by virtue of its two Pratt & Whitney F100-PW-100 turbofan engines, it has the twin fins of many modern aircraft although not variable-geometry wings. The Eagle was first flown on 27 July 1972, subsequent production for the USAF encompassing F-15A and -C single-seaters and F-15B and -D two-seat trainers. Exported Eagles have been delivered to Israel, Saudi Arabia and Japan, although most F-15s for the JASDF (as shown) are licence-built in Japan by Mitsubishi.

▲118

▲119 ▼120

118. The General Dynamics F-16 Fighting Falcon first flew as a prototype on 2 February 1974 and deployment of F-16A single-seat fighters and F-16B two-seat trainers with the USAF began in late 1976 and in 1977 respectively. The F-16 has already attracted major orders from countries around the world, most importantly from Europe – the Netherlands, Belgium, Denmark and Norway – where production is also undertaken. Israeli F-16s were the first to see action, when they took part in the raid on Iraq's Osirak nuclear reactor in 1981. A Dutch F-16 from No. 306 Squadron is illustrated.

119. The latest versions of the F-16 are the F-16C and F-16D, superseding the F-16A and F-16B respectively. All models of this lightweight fighter are each powered by one Pratt & Whitney F100-PW-200 turbofan engine, allowing a speed of over Mach 2. Armament comprises a multi-barrel cannon plus up to six Sidewinders or other weapons, including a massive load for ground attack. F-16s have recently re-equipped the USAF's *Thunderbirds* display team, as shown.

120. Having developed its T-2 trainer, the first supersonic aircraft of Japanese origin, Mitsubishi subsequently put into production for the JASDF a single-seat close-support fighter derivative known as the F-1. The prototype first flew on 3 June 1975, and production aircraft went into service in small numbers from 1977. Each is powered by two Rolls-Royce/Turboméca Adour Mk 801A turbofan engines and armament comprises one multi-barrel cannon and four Sidewinders or attack weapons. This particular aircraft is flown by the 3rd Wing of the JASDF at Misawa. (Ryuta Watanabe)

121. The Dassault-Breguet Mirage 2000 C1 is the latest French single-seat interceptor and air superiority fighter, joining French Air Force units from 1983. A formidable aircraft capable of more than Mach 2.3 on the power of its single SNECMA M53 turbofan and possessing a high rate of climb and excellent manoeuvrability, it is configured as a tailless delta. The first prototype flew on 10 March 1978 and some 200 are expected to join French units as interceptor fighters, with perhaps a similar number later for strike and reconnaissance duties. Armament is two cannon plus four Super 530 and 550 Magic missiles. This Mirage 2000.C1 is engaged in flight refuelling.

121▼

▲122

▲123

122. The outstanding combat aircraft of the Falklands conflict was the BAe Sea Harrier FRS.1, the latest Royal Navy fighter, reconnaissance and strike aircraft that is currently deployed on board *Invincible* class carriers. A V/STOL single-seater developed from the RAF's Harrier and powered by a single Rolls-Royce Pegasus Mk 104 vectored thrust turbofan engine, it has a maximum speed of Mach 1.25 (dived) and is missile-armed with two Sidewinders. The Indian Navy has also received Sea Harriers as Mk 51s, as illustrated, these carrying Magic missiles.
123. From the Mirage III-E, Dassault-Breguet developed the Mirage 5 attack aircraft; from the Mirage III/5 came the Mirage 50 fighter. The initial flight of the Mirage 50 was on 15 April 1979. The aircraft is similar in configuration to the earlier type but uses the powerful SNECMA Atar 9K-50 and can attain Mach 2.2. Chile became the first customer.
124. A Dassault-Breguet aircraft of typical Mirage configuration but larger, twin-engined (two SNECMA M53 turbofans) and supporting foreplanes is the Mach 2.3-plus Super Mirage 4000, a single-seat interceptor and penetration attack aircraft with a rate of climb of 18,300m (60,000ft) per minute. The first flight took place on 9 March 1979, and the aircraft can be armed with two cannon plus up to fourteen missiles in an air combat role. As yet no orders for the Super Mirage 4000 have been announced.
125. From 1985 the RAF will begin deploying a new interceptor fighter to replace its Lightnings and Phantoms – the two-seat swing-wing Tornado F.2. This is a special air defence variant of the multi-national Panavia Tornado combat aircraft, and the RAF, the only customer so far, will eventually receive 165. A Mach 2 aircraft powered by two Turbo Union RB.199-34R Mk 101 turbofan engines, it will carry a cannon plus four Sky Flash and two Sidewinder missiles. The first prototype, as illustrated, flew initially on 27 October 1979.

124▲   125▼

▲126

126. After the Northrop YF-17 prototype lightweight fighter failed to attract USAF orders against the rival F-16, McDonnell Douglas and Northrop collaborated to develop the YF-17 into a new combat plane to meet a US Navy requirement for an A-7 and F-4 replacement. One result of this was the McDonnell Douglas F/A-18 Hornet single-seat carrier-capable strike fighter, which first flew on 18 November 1978 and has since joined the US Navy, the US Marine Corps, the Canadian Armed Forces (as the CF-18), and the Australian and Spanish air forces; exported aircraft are operated from land bases only, as is Northrop's lighter and higher-performance F/A-18L version. Powered by two General Electric F404-GE-400 turbofans, the Hornet (illustrated here in

US Navy markings) has a speed in excess of Mach 1.8 and carries a multi-barrel cannon plus four Sidewinder and Sparrow missiles or other weapons.

127. The newest US fighter is the Northrop F-20 Tigershark. Intended for export, it is based on the company's earlier and highly successful F-5 series but achieves a vastly superior performance by virtue of a single General Electric F404-GE-100 turbofan, an engine which offers much more thrust than the F-5's two smaller engines for little extra weight. It is capable of Mach 2 and is armed with two cannon plus six Sidewinders or other weapons. First flown on 30 August 1982, the F-20 has already been ordered by Bahrain.

▼127